HOME IS ON TOP OF A DOG HOUSE

BY

CHARLES M. SCHULZ

ISBN-13: 978-1-933662-08-4
ISBN-10: 1-933662-08-5

This book may be ordered by mail from the publisher.
Please include $4.50 for postage and handling.
But please support your local bookseller first!

Books published by Cider Mill Press Book Publishers are available at special discounts for bulk purchases in the United States by corporations, institutions, and other organizations. For more information, please contact the publisher.

Cider Mill Press Book Publishers
"Where good books are ready for press"
12 Port Farm Road
Kennebunkport, Maine 04046

Visit us on the web!
www.cidermillpress.com

Design by: Jason Zamajtuk

Printed in China

3 4 5 6 7 8 9 10

A PEANUTS CLASSIC Edition

HOME
IS ON TOP OF A DOG HOUSE

Outer
space
fascinates
me.

Show me a veterinarian, and I'll show you a man who loves to wield a needle!

I love
to hear the
patter of rain
on the roof
while
I'm
sleeping.

Snow
is
nice
too.

There's the ugliest sight in the world...an empty dog dish!

On a clear night I can get Mexico City.

I miss Mr. Peepers.

Some guys never really learn to do anything.

It is
my humble
opinion that
a night's sleep
dreaming of cats
is no
night's sleep
at all.

The only time I hear from the Daisy Hill Puppy Farm Alumni Association is when they want another donation!

How can you do push-ups when your nose gets in the way?

I always have a few friends over for Bridge on Thursdays.

NO TRUMP

About five minutes of this is all I can take... then I get claustrophobia!

Commuter!

What do you do when your National Geographics begin to overflow?

Is

it

fall

already?

I live
in constant fear
that someone
will break in
and
steal all of my
Hank Williams
records.

So.

what's wrong

with

having

a

night

light?

What
terrible luck...
I plan a picnic
for today,
and
what happens?
A locust
plague!

There's nothing like having a friend at the Army Surplus store.

Rats!
Someone left
the
light on
over
the
pool table!

I think I'm allergic to morning.

"Pigeons in the grass alas. Beagle on the roof aloof!"

I hate windy days.

Who
else
do you know
who
can do
the
"Beagle"?

Actually,
all I did
was put this
sweet potato
in a jar
of water, see...
and...
well...

Everyone should spend at least one night during the summer camping out.

Have
you
ever had
one of those days
when you felt
you just had
to bite someone
on the leg?

The
worst part
about living alone
is not having
someone
to bring you
tea and toast
at
bedtime.

I do a lot of complaining, but actually I love my home!

About Cider Mill Press Book Publishers

Good ideas ripen with time. From seed to harvest, Cider Mill Press strives to bring fine reading, information, and entertainment together between the covers of its creatively crafted books. Our Cider Mill bears fruit twice a year, publishing a new crop of titles each Spring and Fall.

Visit us on the web at
www.cidermillpress.com
or write to us at
12 Port Farm Road
Kennebunkport, Maine 04046

CIDER MILL PRESS
BOOK PUBLISHERS

Where Good Books are Ready for Press